Tracy McGrady

by John Hareas

23018

SCHOLASTIC INC.
New York   Toronto   London   Auckland   Sydney
Mexico City   New Delhi   Hong Kong   Buenos Aires

To my newest and precious All-Star, Leah Catherine Hareas — J.H.

PHOTO CREDIT

All images copyright NBAE/Getty Images
(1) Bill Baptist; (3) Glenn James; (5) Jennifer Pottheiser; (7) Thanks to
the McGrady family; (9) Craig Jones; (10) Andy Hayt; (12, 14) Fernando
Medina; (15) Mitchell Layton; (17) Ron Turenne; (19) Ron Hoskins; (19)
Ron Hoskins; (21) Bill Baptist; (22) Layne Murdoch; (23) Nathaniel S. Butler

ISBN 0-439-78803-X

12 11 10 9 8 7 6 5 4 3 2   6 7 8 9 10/0

Printed in the U.S.A.
First printing, January 2006
Book Design: Angela Jun

Contents

Meet Tracy McGrady

Tracy McGrady dreamed of playing professional sports, but instead of shooting jumpers, he wanted to throw fastballs just like pitcher Dwight Gooden.

Tracy grew up in Auburndale, Florida, a small town between Orlando and Tampa. He was a Little League All-Star and had shelves of home run balls and team trophies to prove it. But by the time McGrady reached high school, he was close to 6–4 — and he kept growing. When he graduated, Tracy was 6–8 and one of the top *basketball* prospects in the country. Dreams of being a great baseball

star were replaced by dreams of becoming the next NBA superstar.

In the 1996 NBA Draft, McGrady was chosen by the Toronto Raptors and joined his cousin Vince Carter who also played there. In Toronto, McGrady had to make a big adjustment — on and off the court. He played well alongside his "Cuz" but after three seasons in Toronto, he felt he was ready to lead his own team, and he returned to Florida, joining the Orlando Magic. His game took off. Suddenly, Tracy was one of the NBA's best all-around players. With jaw-dropping dunks, three-pointers, and mid-range jumpers, he became one of the NBA's premier scorers and put the league on notice. Not only did he win the NBA's Most Improved Player honors but he also won back-to-back scoring titles. He became the youngest player to average 30-plus points per game since the NBA absorbed three ABA teams in 1976.

Fans and teammates were blown away by the new and improved McGrady.

"I knew he could play, but he's so much better than I thought," said Grant Hill of the Magic. "This kid's a star. You could see he really stepped up and answered the call. This is his time."

McGrady eventually took his All-Star talents to Houston, where he has teamed up with another

All-Star, center Yao Ming. McGrady and Yao are one of the league's most feared dynamic duos. Not only did McGrady lead the Rockets in scoring in 2004–05, averaging 25.7 points, but he continued to wow fans with his athleticism and scoring ability. In one game, McGrady put on one of the greatest one-man scoring shows in league history. With the visiting San Antonio Spurs up by 10 points and little more than one minute to go, T-Mac heated up. The four-time All-Star sank four three-pointers, including one with 1.7 seconds left to give the Rockets an 81–80 win. McGrady ended up scoring 13 points in just 35 seconds!

Fans admire T-Mac's talents — that's why he's voted to the NBA All-Star team every season. His No. 1 Houston Rockets jersey was the second-most-popular jersey in the NBA during the 2004–05 season. Off the court, the laid-back McGrady loves to give back. Whether it's in Florida or Houston, McGrady always makes time for charities and the NBA's Read to Achieve program. In 2003, McGrady was named one of the "Good Guys in Sports" by *The Sporting News*. When it comes to fun, Tracy loves to ride his dirt bikes and jet skis, play video games, or jump on the trampoline he has at his house. He also likes to sleep. His nickname is the Big Sleep. He can take a nap anywhere, anytime.

Growing Up

Tracy Lamar McGrady was born on May 24, 1979, in Bartow, Fla., a small, friendly, Southern community. He grew up in a neighboring town called Auburndale, located in Polk County, with a population of 11,000 people. At age five, McGrady was already playing sports. You name it, he played it — baseball, football, basketball. His first organized sport was T-ball. He played in the Auburndale Little League, and he would soon become an Auburndale Little League All-Star — twice.

"That was my No. 1 love right there," said McGrady. "I started playing baseball at age five. I started out pitching and I used to throw a lot of junk pitches. That kind of messed up my arm as I got older."

McGrady wanted to be able to pitch like his boyhood hero, Cy Young-winner and Tampa Bay native, Doc Gooden.

But Tracy was also starting to develop his love

for basketball, playing on city courts with his next-door neighbor and cousin, Phillip Richardson.

As he entered his teens, Tracy had a growth spurt. He grew 12 inches from ages 12 to 17! By the time he attended Auburndale High School, he was approaching 6-4 and still growing. By the time Tracy entered his junior year, he was already 6-7. And it was during his junior year that Tracy started showing flashes of his terrific basketball skills. As a sophomore, he averaged 16.2 points. In his junior year, he averaged 23.1 points. His coach, Ty Willis, said that Tracy dunked 60 times in his junior season.

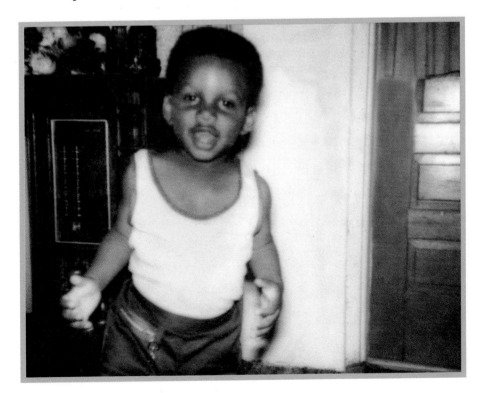

After playing baseball in his freshman and junior years, Tracy decided to drop the sport and focus on basketball. Tracy left Auburndale High School to attend Mount Zion Christian Academy, a school located in North Carolina. The competition at Mount Zion was better and, as good a player as he was, Tracy was still an unknown on the national level.

But before he began at Mount Zion, Tracy visited a top prep high school camp in the country, called the ABCD, located in Teaneck, N.J. Tracy truly arrived at this camp. If people hadn't heard about Tracy McGrady before, they did now. He starred, dominating the competition, and picked up MVP honors. The unknown had become an overnight sensation.

Tracy entered Mount Zion on a roll. He continued to wow the competition and the growing number of college scouts who were now interested in this hot prospect. He earned tournament MVP honors while leading Mount Zion to a 26–2 record, averaging 27.5 points, 8.7 rebounds, and 7.7 assists during his senior season. Suddenly, the player who hadn't been among the top 500 prospects in the nation, was listed No. 2 overall. People weren't just talking about college for Tracy, many were thinking NBA.

Hello, NBA

T racy collected all the major awards during his senior season at Mount Zion. He was named *USA Today* Player of the Year and North Carolina state Player of the Year by the *Associated Press*. He also was named to the McDonald's All-America Team.

Word spread and all of the major colleges were trying to recruit him, but the chance to play in the

NBA and provide for his family was too good to pass up. Tracy felt he would be a lottery pick — a top-13 selection — in the NBA Draft, and he was right. The Toronto Raptors selected Tracy with the 9th

overall pick. His dreams of playing in the NBA would come true.

Having joined the NBA in 1995, the Toronto Raptors were a new franchise. The team was trying to make the playoffs, and after seasons of 21 and 30 victories, the Raptors were hoping that the improvement would continue. Unfortunately, the team went backward during Tracy's rookie season. Head coach Darrell Walker was released after 49 games and replaced by Butch Carter. The Raptors won only 16 games that season and lost 66. For Tracy, life in the NBA was difficult — on and off the court. On the court, he averaged only 7 points and 18.4 minutes per game. He also found that NBA players were bigger and quicker than he was used to. Plus, he was homesick. Toronto is a long way from Auburndale.

However, things looked up after that first season. In a trade with the Golden State Warriors, the Raptors acquired Vince Carter, an All-American out of the University of North Carolina. Vince and Tracy knew each other from Florida. And it turned out that they were distant cousins. They called each other "Cuz." Now the Raptors were on the move. The team won 23 games in the shortened 50-game NBA season and 45 the next season. Vince won NBA Rookie of the Year honors on his way to

superstardom. He dazzled fans worldwide, winning the NBA Slam Dunk title in 2000 and became the leader of the much-improved Raptors. Tracy's game also improved. He went from averaging 9.3 points to 15.4 as he started the last half of the season.

That season (1999–2000) not only saw Tracy elevate his game but the Raptors made the NBA Playoffs for the first time in franchise history. Even though the Raptors were swept by the New York Knicks, Tracy sparkled, averaging 17 points and 7 assists per game.

The future looked bright for Toronto *and* for Tracy. He had started to grow and develop into one of the league's rising stars, and he and Vince were one of the NBA's most dynamic duos. Tracy once again was faced with a huge decision. His three-year contract was up. Would he stay with the Raptors and his "Cuz," or play for any team he wanted to become the main man?

Going Home

Only three years out of high school, Tracy again found himself in demand. NBA teams lined up, hoping to convince the 20-year-old to play for them. Tracy wasn't the only top free agent: Tim Duncan and Grant Hill also headlined the class of available players.

The Chicago Bulls and Miami Heat tried to sign McGrady, but in the end it was the Orlando Magic

15

who signed Tracy to a six-year contract. The Magic are based in Orlando, a 45-minute drive from Auburndale. Not only would Tracy be close to his family and friends, he would be in a situation that could showcase his skills. The Magic were big winners that summer because they signed Grant Hill as well.

Everyone in central Florida was excited about the possibilities of the Hill-McGrady combination. Unfortunately, Magic fans only saw a glimpse of this duo's potential. After playing only four games together, Hill had season-ending ankle surgery. It was Tracy's time to step up, and the league took notice. Tracy earned All-Star honors and was among the NBA's leading scorers, averaging 26.8 points per game. He also won the NBA's Most Improved Player Award. Tracy led the Magic to the playoffs and led the league in postseason scoring with a 33.8-point average.

"I guess I'm the go-to guy," McGrady said. "That's all right; that's my job. Until Grant gets healthy, I'm up to playing a bigger role."

Off the court, Tracy played a large role as well. T-Mac established the Tracy McGrady Foundation and donated more than $350,000 to various children's charities. He also donated generously to Auburndale High School and Mount Zion Christian

Academy. *The Sporting News* named Tracy as one of its "Good Guys in Sports," and he was given the top community honor by the Magic — the Rich and Helen DeVos Community Enrichment Award — for his outstanding community service.

While Grant Hill continued to suffer ankle problems during the 2001–02 season, playing in only 14 games, Tracy soared. T-Mac averaged 25.8 points per game and once again was named to the Eastern Conference All-Star team.

Unfortunately for Tracy and the Magic, Hill's ankle problems continued. He played in only 29 games in the 2002–03 season and missed the entire 2003–04 season. Tracy once again carried the team on his back, leading the league in scoring both seasons — but he needed help. Tracy couldn't do it alone. The Magic would reach the playoffs only to lose in the first round. Tracy was getting frustrated and so were the fans.

Off the court, Tracy continued to make a difference. He befriended a 13-year-old boy, Iran Brown, who was injured in the Washington-area sniper shootings. When Tracy found out that he was Iran's favorite athlete, he not only sent him a box of jerseys and other basketball memorabilia, he invited the boy and his family to a Magic game.

When Iran was healthy enough to attend a game, there was a chance Tracy wouldn't play since he missed three consecutive games with a lower back strain. Tracy not only played but he scored 46 points and led the Magic to a victory. Tracy didn't want to disappoint his new friend.

"I had my man Iran here," said McGrady after the game.

The hope and optimism of the summer of 2000 never became reality for Magic fans. The McGrady-Hill combo never got off the ground. McGrady suffered through his worst NBA season in 2003–04. The Magic started the season at 1–19 and finished with the worst record in the NBA at 21–61.

Tracy had been in the NBA for seven years and he still wasn't any closer to a championship. After four years in Orlando, the Magic decided to trade him. As part of a blockbuster seven-player trade that included All-Star point guard Steve Francis, who went to the Magic, Tracy would now get a chance to win a championship ring with his new team, the Houston Rockets.

The fans in Houston were thrilled about the two-time NBA scoring champion joining All-Star center Yao Ming on their team. On June 30, 2004, thousands of fans waited in the pouring rain to enter the Toyota Center and welcome the

four-time All-Star at his first-ever Rockets press conference.

"It choked me up," said McGrady of the large turnout. "It really did. When you see things like that, you can't help but get emotional, because if it wasn't for the fans, we wouldn't be who we are. We've just got to give back."

Hopes were high in Houston among the fans and the team. Unfortunately, the Rockets sputtered to a 6–11 start, but after a series of trades involving point guards, the Rockets were finally airborne. The team won 12 of their next 16 games. While Tracy's focus was on wins, and not scoring titles,

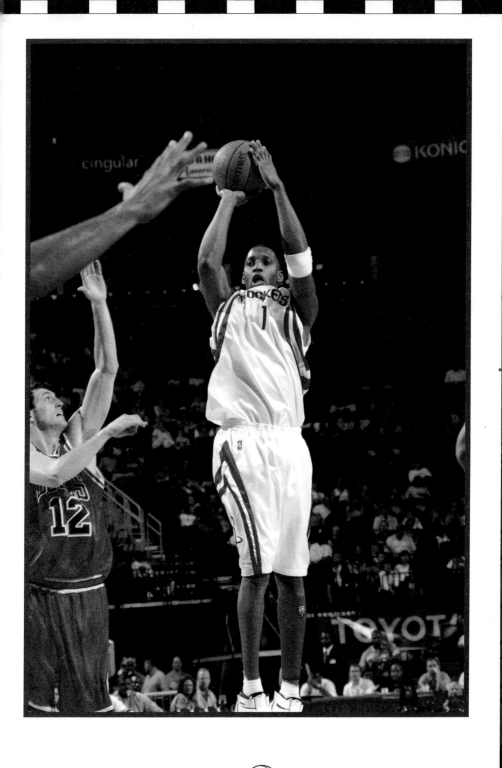

he did put on more than a few spectacular scoring displays. There was the game against the San Antonio Spurs when T-Mac came to the rescue. Another time, Tracy scored 48 points while Dirk Nowitzki dropped in 53 in a regular-season game between the Rockets and the Dallas Mavericks.

The Rockets headed into the 2005 playoffs on a roll, winning 10 of their last 14 games. The Rockets faced the Mavericks in the first round and, after winning the first two games, they looked like a cinch to advance. But the Mavs stormed back, winning the next three games and taking the series in a deciding seventh game.

For McGrady and the Rockets, this disappointment stung. This was the fifth time in Tracy's career that his team did not advance past the first round.

"I'm not going to hang my head," said McGrady. "I'm 25 years old and I've got a lot more years in this league, and I will be back next year. All of this that I'm going through is only going to make me tougher. I will never fold regardless of being bounced out of the first round for four or five years. I won't fold and I will be back and my team will be back. We will be back, better and stronger."

There isn't any doubt that the best is yet to come for Tracy, Yao, and the Rockets.

Read to Achieve

This year, NBA Players
and Coaches are continuing
to share their words...

And by promoting reading and on-line literacy,
they are spreading the word that every child
should have the chance to *Read to Achieve*.

FOR MORE INFORMATION ON READ TO ACHIEVE,
LOG ON TO NBA.com.